Rainforests
Grow So High

KINGFISHER

NEW YORK

KINGFISHER
LONDON & NEW YORK

Copyright © Kingfisher 2012
Published in the United States by Kingfisher,
175 Fifth Ave., New York, NY 10010
Kingfisher is an imprint of Macmillan Children's Books, London.
All rights reserved.

Written and designed by Dynamo Ltd.

Distributed in the U.S. and Canada by Macmillan,
175 Fifth Ave., New York, NY 10010

Library of Congress Cataloging-in-Publication data has been applied for.

ISBN 978-0-7534-7004-6

Kingfisher books are available for special promotions and premiums. For details contact:
Special Markets Department, Macmillan, 175 Fifth Ave., New York, NY 10010.

For more information, please visit www.kingfisherbooks.com

Printed in China
9 8 7 6 5 4 3 2 1
1TR/0612/HH/-/140MA

Contents

Why do rainforests grow so high?

Rainforests are jungles that grow near the equator, an imaginary line around the middle of Earth.

The jungle grows very thick, and the trees must grow high to reach the sunlight.

All about rainforests

- In rainforest areas, the weather is warm and it rains for a little while every day.
- The world's biggest rainforest spreads around the Amazon River in South America.
- Some rainforest trees grow up to 130 ft. (40m) high.

It rains
very hard in
the rainforest

5

Which animals live in rainforests?

Rainforests are home to more than half of all the types of animals and plants on Earth.

Many of the animals live up in the trees.

Rainforest animals

- Rainforests can be noisy places, with birds squawking and monkeys howling.
- Under the trees, there is a thick layer of dead leaves called leaf litter.
- Ants and beetles live in the leaf litter.

The Amazon rainforest

Monkeys and birds live in the trees

Many insects and frogs live here, too

What is there to eat among the trees?

Many rainforest animals eat juicy fruit and nuts from the trees and bushes.

Some creatures spend their time hunting other animals to eat.

Rainforest food

- Some insects and birds drink the sweet nectar from flowers.
- Rainforest monkeys swing between the trees, searching for food.
- Some creatures come out only at night to feed. They are called nocturnal animals.

A little cotton-top
tamarin eats fruit
from an Amazon tree

9

Do people live in rainforests?

Small tribes (groups) of people live in some of the world's rainforests. They gather plants from the forest and hunt animals to eat.

They build huts out of the forest branches and leaves.

Rainforest people

- The Amazon people make medicine using the plants they find.
- They build their own canoes to go fishing on the river.
- They make their own tools and clothes.

Some Amazon
hunters use
arrows tipped
with poison

They make the
poison from
forest plants

11

Which rainforest plants grow underwater?

The Amazon rainforest has several rivers and lakes. Water plants, such as giant water lilies, grow on them.

The water lilies have their roots in the riverbed. They grow up to the surface, and their leaves float on top of the water.

Water plants

- Fish swim around under the leaves of the water plants.
- Giant water lily leaves are strong enough for a small child to sit on.
- Water lily flowers grow up to 12 in. (30cm) wide. They smell like pineapple.

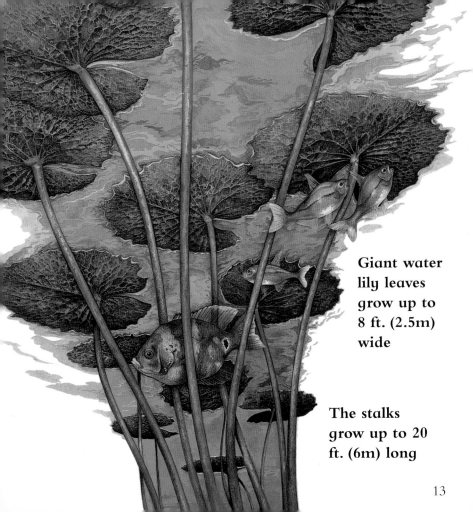

Giant water
lily leaves
grow up to
8 ft. (2.5m)
wide

The stalks
grow up to 20
ft. (6m) long

13

What flies in the rainforest?

All kinds of birds live in the rainforest trees. In the Amazon, you might see macaws with brightly colored feathers flying around.

The macaws have tough beaks for cracking open nuts.

Rainforest birds

- Macaws eat the fruit, nuts, and seeds that they find in the treetops.
- Macaws live together in noisy flocks.
- Some rainforest birds hunt other creatures to eat. They are called birds of prey.

14

This hornbill has long claws for gripping onto tree branches

macaw

What swims through the Amazon?

The Amazon rainforest is crisscrossed with rivers full of underwater creatures.

There are many different fish, swimming snakes, and even a type of small crocodile called a caiman.

Capybara drinking at the water's edge

Caiman

Piranha

Anaconda

17

What is it like to visit a rainforest?

A rainforest is a hot, steamy place—and rather dark, too. Giant trees tower overhead, blocking out the light below.

There are probably many creatures and plants yet to be discovered in the depths of the rainforest.

Visiting the Amazon

- You can travel into the Amazon rainforest on a riverboat.

- It would be easy to get lost in the rainforest without a guide.

- You would need to be careful of dangers, such as stinging insects and biting snakes.

Scientists visit
rainforests to
study them

19

Why do rainforests need to be saved?

Thousands of acres of rainforest trees are chopped down every day to be used as logs.

One day the rainforest could disappear, along with the animals and plants that live there.

Why are rainforests important?

- Some important medicines are made from rainforest plants.

- If the rainforests disappear, it is possible that Earth's weather could be affected.

- Millions of animals would lose their homes and die out if the rainforests were destroyed.

Rare and beautiful animals and plants are under threat

21

What do you know about rainforests?

You can find all of the answers to these questions in this book.

Can you name a type of animal that lives in a rainforest?

Where is the world's biggest rainforest?

Do you think rainforest people live in apartment buildings or huts?

Do you think it
is warm or cold
in a rainforest?

Would you like to
visit a rainforest
one day?

Some rainforest words

Equator The imaginary line around the middle of Earth.

Flock A group of birds living together.

Leaf litter A layer of dead leaves covering the floor of a rainforest.

Nectar Sweet liquid inside a flower.

Nocturnal Animals that come out at night.

Prey Animals that are hunted and eaten by other animals.

Tribe A group of people who live together.